Been There Done That!

Keeping Your Sanity While

SINGLE PARENTING

COLLETTE CONNER

ILLUSTRATD BY

VICTOR J. GADDIE

Been There Done That

Copyright © 2018 by Collette T. Conner

All rights reserved.

Publisher:

Collette Conner

ctconner100@gmail.com

Publishing consultant:

Professional Woman Publishing, LLC

www.pwnbooks.com

Illustrated by Victor J. Gaddie

ISBN: 978-0-578-21058-2

CONTENTS

Introduction 1

Chapter One: Say It Ain't So 7

Chapter Two: The Reality Of It All 19

Chapter Three: No Plan, It's Ok 29

Chapter Four: Pick Your Battles 39

Chapter Five: Calling Forth Greatness 55

Chapter SIX: Don't Panic In The Pain 67

Chapter Seven: Loving When You Need Love The Most 77

Chapter Eight: Remembering The Big (P) "Purpose" 87

Chapter Nine: Let Go And Let God 97

Chapter Ten: The Case For Thesingle Parent 119

Letter From The Desk Of The Author 125

About The Author 127

Introduction

The first example of a single parent I knew of or had experienced was my mother and grandmother. They were my first view into the life of a single parent. There were no adult male examples in the house that would offer manly wisdom or give us memories of what a man really looks like. But somehow, I seemed to have a great childhood.

I remember that even though we did not have much and I was not in a traditional family, I was still free to explore as a child without the cares of the world.

Even though single parenthood existed back then, it was just a drop in the bucket compared to the number of households that experience it today.

According to the U.S. Census Bureau, there are over eleven million single-parent family households today. Over seventeen million children under the age of eighteen are being raised without a father. More than eighty percent of single-parent households are headed by single mothers. The Median Income for single mothers is below $36,000 compared to that of the median income for married couples being above $85,000.

As we all know, there are single-parent homes that do not fit in the median and live well below these statistics who struggle every day to make ends meet and provide for their family.

Many single-parent households are forced to live off one income, which means resources and time are stretched to the limit.

It means that time is now divided into fractions of time to meet the needs of others. It means that the weight of all responsibility to ensure that everyone in their household is a success is primarily on one person's shoulders. Whether that means being a success on the soccer field, in the classroom, or just simply a success at being a good person.

Single parenthood is one of the most, if not the most, challenging tasks anyone could ever undertake. Why do I think this? I have been there and done that. This is why I feel lead to encourage, challenge, and inspire single parents to stay in the race and never give up. Don't give up on yourself or on your child or children.

Single parenting means that there is one person, a sole body, doing all the parenting in that household. You run all the errands, cook all the meals, do all the shopping, the laundry, all the discipline, and so on. I know that there are exceptions when someone else may help out here and there, a friend, family or even an older child. However, for the most part, single means single, which is one.

I want to encourage you to take one day at a time and understand that when you think you've come to the end of your rope, tie a knot and hold on for dear life. You will get through it. When it seems like no one understands you or your actions because they can't see and don't know your purpose or the big picture, just smile and keep moving.

Surviving seasons of single parenthood has taught me to hold on in the tough times because things will get better. No matter what it looks like, stay encouraged because seasons change. This book speaks to the single woman as well as the single man. Both will experience the ups and downs of single parenthood. This book does not focus on the statistics even though they are mentioned. Still, its focus is sending the message you can overcome the staggering statistics. It encourages single parents to go through it and still have your right mind? How to get it done and not lose yourself. How to live through the disappointments and letdowns.

I want to challenge you to stand firm in the power of God's might. Stand firm in knowing that you were made in His image, and so are the child or children that are in your care. Remember that God has a specific purpose for their lives as well as yours. He knew that he built you to last through these challenging eighteen-plus years.

Yes, I said plus years for all you parents who say to yourself," I can't wait till this child turns eighteen." News flash, it does not stop there. God will be with you every step of the way. From your child's first steps to their first drive behind the wheel.

The challenge is for every single parent to know is that it is ok not to be perfect because no one is. That your children are not all the time going to get you. And by the way, they will let you know what they don't get. Believe me. Most of all, the challenge for single parents is to not lose yourself in the process because one day, for some, sooner than others, they will be able to stand on their own, and you will be left with that person where it all began, you. So always hold on to you, even if it means holding on to little pieces of you.

I want to inspire you to never give up on yourself. Never give up on the one who has made all of this happen, you. Never give up on your dreams and the things that God had placed inside of you from the very beginning. You know those things that were there before you had kids and had to go at it all alone. Sure, you may have had to place it on hold, or you may have to tweak it here and there. You may even have to totally strategize it all together but never completely throw it in the trash.

God uses everything. He uses every experience that you go through. I like to say that he uses the good, the bad, and the ugly. He throws nothing away. He is just that perfect and purposeful. So be inspired to soar above any obstacles that come your way as a single parent. And believe me, single parenthood will bring plenty of obstacles. But with you and your invisible partner, God, you can get the job done.

Looking at all the statistics, someone may ask the question, "Is there anything good that can come out of single parenting?"

This book will humor you and inspire you as I lead you on a journey of faith through the pages. It will give you another perspective on what single parenthood is and what it can be. I believe that this book is different from others on single parenthood because it captures the essence of God's plans for our lives. It shows us that life is challenging, but we are overcomers.

"I've Been There, Done That" (Keeping Your Sanity, While Single Parenting) is meant to simply give you some insight into what you may be facing as a parent that finds themselves dealing with the many facets of raising a child or children alone. I have lived through all of it, the good, the bad, and the ugly. After reading this book, I pray that you will be inspired to hope, empowered to win, and challenged to get the job done in excellence.

CHAPTER ONE

Say It Ain't So

*M*arriage is supposed to mean partnership and should bring along with it a support system that is in the best interest of the child or children. It is protection magnesium for the family unit. That thing which seals the family together. However, the family as we know it is under attack. The family unit has taken a major shift in the past years.

The traditional family has changed drastically, and many households are being headed by single parents who are moms. So this dream of a lasting, blissful marriage has been diminished. It is not what a lot of us had hoped for. Now I am only speaking of those who get as far as marriage. I have not yet tapped into the whole baby mama drama syndrome.

So here you are, and your plans did not work out the way you had planned them. Ok, it didn't work out, and you are left to do it alone. You are now officially a single parent. Some of you may have had a significant other or ex do their part—picking up the kids on their weekends and so forth.

They may even be faithful at paying their child support but make no mistake about it, you are still left with having to do all of that plus more. You have financial obligations; you have to do most of the day-to-day running for the household and deal with the emotional tug of war with the kids.

Getting some support on any level is far better than not getting any at all. I am a witness. When you get no support, or your support is so inconsistent that it feels like no support, things are so much harder on you as a single parent, and that brings me to another point.

God will give grace to those single parents who really get no ongoing support at all. No child support check, no weekends off, no help with errands, no emotional support, etc.

Have you ever thought to yourself, "How did I get here?" Say it ain't so. The truth in the matter is that many roads lead to the city called single parenthood. So that is not my concern in writing this book.

My goal is to inspire, encourage, and empower those who find themselves playing the role of a single parent. Now, this is not just any role; it is the starting role. Oh, I forgot to tell you that even though you have the starting role, there is no personal makeup artist and no personal stylist. There is no celebrity hairstylist, no power lunches or remakes of scenes. Oh yeah, and no one screaming, "CUT."

I want to empower you to walk single parenthood out in excellence. Notice I did not say perfection. Excellence is the quality of being outstanding or extremely good in a given situation. Remember when you have done your very best, given all factors in your life, and you have exhausted all resources, then you have done excellently.

As I said, this does not mean you are perfect or will do things perfectly. Perfect means faultless, flawless, and absolutely complete. See the difference. Being a single parent does not require you to be perfect. It just requires you to be there in the way your child or children requires you to be there.

Now I am not saying that there are not times when your children expect you to be perfect. Like being able to leap tall buildings in a single bound with groceries and laundry strapped to your back. Yes, you're sometimes expected to be superwoman or superman even when you feel as if you need rescuing. So here lies the overall challenge.

Been There Done That

To be excellent without trying to be perfect. Perfection is pretty much a lie within itself. Ask yourself, can it truly be obtained, and if not, why waste time in its arena. However, excellence is obtainable. For example, in raising my kids, I made every effort to direct them in getting an education because I knew it would be their stepping stone out of the statistics that could plague them.

I let them know that it was important because one day, they would be head of households that would consist of a wife and children who would be dependent on them. They understood that college was one of those paths to their dreams. So with help, they made an effort to get there, and now, two of them are college graduates—just one less thing to worry about. Now my youngest son is in college, but his heart has always been the heart of an entrepreneur. We have all heard the saying, "When life gives you lemons, make lemonade." When you find yourself single and alone raising kids, whether you are a mom, a dad, or a grandmother raising your children's children, remember that lemons don't have to stay bitterly tart.

Add a little sugar here and there, mix things up and one day, you will be able to sit back in the cool of the shade and drink lemonade. Even if that shade is just knowing that you survived that season of your life and still have you. Even if that lemonade is just a cool drink of contentment. Knowing that you not only survived it, but you walked it out in excellence in the face of all your obstacles, with all your flaws and faults.

So you have gotten over the initial shock of singleness when it relates to raising your children. You understand that things going forward will forever be changed, and your way of doing things will forever be changing for the betterment of the family. You are now the primary provider, nurturer, and disciplinary tutor and guide.

Looking back at my school days, I remember aspiring, at that time, to be an attorney and imagining what my life would be like when I grew up. Single parenthood never made its way into not one single thought. It's funny how life happens.

When you don't take full control of it and become part of someone else's plan. In so many ways, we are all a part of someone else's plan being it voluntarily or involuntarily. Just make sure that your plan is front and center.

I am not talking about selfishness at all, but I am talking about being true to you. In short, life sometimes does happen, but the happenings of life do not have to control the rest of your life. Thank God for redemption! Let what happened in your past be a "Do not do guide" for your future.

Life is just that; it happens. It's real, and it sometimes is a surprise and out of your control. Other times it is a direct result of the choices we make. Life is living, and if it is living, it has the potential to change. To renew, to be restored, refreshed and rejuvenated.

Romans 8:28

And we know these things work together for good of them that love God, to them who are called according to his purpose.

If people really believed this scripture, they would not be so quick to fall into a spiral of hopelessness because they are experiencing the ugly life. They would say to themselves, this is not happening to me but would hold on to the end of the rope, believing that something good has to come out of a bad situation. So they find the strength to stick it out and see the good.

Everybody will go through ups and downs, but as a single parent, especially a single mom, it seems your downs may out weight your ups. Just think, the most, if not all, the load of raising a child is on you.

At the end of the day, you are where the buck stops. If it's to be done, then you have to do it. If there is a hero needed, then you are that hero. If someone is down in the dumps and needs to be motivated out, you are that motivational speaker. So you might as well be in it to win it.

I decided to make the most out of my years as a single mom. I decided to give the most of me so that I could get the job done. Notice I said the most of me, which was an extreme lot. I didn't say all of me because all of me would have left me bitter.

Single parents must remember that God has plans for them too. Those plans may be delayed due to responsibilities but keeping your sanity is needed to fulfill what he has for you.

There will be days of disappointments, struggles and tears. However, to see them grow from boys was so rewarding that it seemed to cancel out some of the tedious processes to get them there. Sure it caused me to put off some self-gratifying desires that I had, but that was all part of the sacrifice.

Now we are all different, and you may be one of those people who can burn both ends of the candle, so be it. If you were wired in such a way that you can leap tall buildings at a single bound, then do so. I truly believe that we can be all things, just not at the same time. There is no use in wallowing over, 'it isn't so' when your reality is so.

The question is what you are going to do about it. There are lives and destinies hanging in the balance. And guess what? You are the chief influencer. You are the Conductor of the train. You may be asking yourself, "Do I have what it takes to get the job done?" Remember you came here equipped for every task in your life.

What you need to get the job done is already in you. What you need to influence the next generation is already there. And if there is something that you feel you don't have, just pray and ask for it. You will either develop it, or it will come by way of someone else. Being a single parent is not all trouble. There will be many rewarding, funny, amazing days also. Reach for those days because they are special. So whether you are a single parent for the first time or have been at it for years, just know it can be done.

When I say it can be done, I am a living witness. When I say I've been there and done that, I have. I have felt your pain and your struggles because I have walked in your shoes.

I know what it is like to have your back against the wall and not know if you can make something happen for your family. I know what it is like to be responsible for having to keep everything going in a positive direction even when you are in a negative situation.

I have been there, and that is why I am more than qualified to encourage you, challenge you, and inspire you to stay in the race. What race? The race to pour into your children everything that they will need to get to the next level. I call it the first years out of the blocks.

Once your children graduate high school, once they are that age, then your day-to-day influence decrease. They are now out the blocks. Making more decisions on their own and your reach of influence is not as effective no matter how great or excellent you think you are.

Up until now, a large degree of everything taught has come from you. Now they have more options. They are out the blocks, other things may influence them, and home is not the only influencer. Take a deep breath, parents; remember, you were the chief influencer. A lot of those values that may be buried underneath the culture, peer pressure and selfish desires are still there.

So while they are still in the blocks, give it all that you got. All that you have may be more or less than what the next parent has to give. Stay in your lane, focused on the race. These years fly by quickly, so learn how to maximize your time and efforts. And most of all don't forget to laugh a lot.

This is one of the most important ingredients to keeping your sanity while single parenting. Why laugh? Because there will be times when you're all cried out and laughing is all you can do. And when you smile, your children smile.

Been There Done That

Make a decision to walk this thing out and see what the end, which could very well be your beginning, will be. Remember, life is an experience that prepares you to help someone else through their experience.

Facing the Music
Chapter 1 Reflections
'Say It ain't So'

How did you feel the moment you realized that you had to raise your children alone? Please share your feelings.

(e.g., alone, scared)

1._____

2._____

3._____

4._____

Now that you have gotten over the shock of having to raise your children on your own, do you have a vision for how you want to raise them? If so, write the vision.

(e.g., value driven, academic driven)

1._____

2._____

3._____

4._____

Been There Done That

How are you going to accomplish the plans you have for your family?

(e.g., extra curriculum activities, church)

1._____

2._____

3._____

4._____

CHAPTER TWO

The Reality of It All

S o let's be real. It is what it is. You are now a single parent, like it or not. Now, do you decide to work on turning lemons into lemonade, or do you let the lemons sour even more? The choice is yours. However you got here, you are here. So what are you going to make of it? It's been said that life is not what happens to you but how you react to what happens to you.

There are only two kinds of people. Those who complain about their circumstances and those who conquer their circumstances. Here is what I mean. Many people try to relieve their adverse situations by giving birth to them every time they open their mouths. They spend valuable time telling everybody they know and even some they don't know, all of their hardships and trials. They tell people who have no intention of helping them or people who just can't help them.

Then there are those who choose to take that same energy and direct it toward strategies that will change their situation. These people can be dealing with the same or similar things, but their perspective, their outlook is different. Perspective is everything.

For example, some would say it is half empty when you look at a glass of water, and some would say it is half full. It is all about perspective. It is your attitude toward a thing, how you regard that thing, a point of view. If you survey a thousand people, you may get a thousand points of view. Therefore your life experiences and your mindset determine your perspective. When raising children, all of this plays a huge part in what type of adults they will be.

Ephesians 1:6

Train up a child in the way he should go and when he is old he will not depart from it.

The Message Bible version says it like this

Point your kids in the right direction and when they are old they won't be lost.

Say It Ain't So

Well, we know that things happen, and when they get old enough to make their own decisions, they will. But that training is still with them. It never leaves them as they go through life, even though some of the decisions they make may not reflect it. Believe me, from time to time, their mind travels back. Our experience as a child, good or bad, is with us. It is part of why we are who we are. It is the reason we make some of the decisions we make or have made. It makes up our perspective. The reality is that as single parents, we are helping to shape the perspective of our children. Wow! That is powerful. We help shape how they see things and make decisions.

We are not responsible for all their actions, but we do have a hand in the way they look at life. This is why if you tell a child that he or she can't do something or that they will not amount to anything, day in and day out, they probably won't. On the other hand, if you tell a child that they can accomplish anything and their possibilities are limitless, they will soar.

So when I talk about turning your sour situation into a sweet one, single parents have the power to do just that. The unfavorable thing that led you here can't keep you here. It can be turned around to favor you. Children are a blessing from the Lord. I know that popular culture may say different, but they are. Single parenthood is an opportunity to totally pour all your love, positive energy, and guidance into a child. Take hold of where you are at in your life and raise your kids on purpose.

Raising your kids on purpose means developing a strategy that works for your household, not what works for Aunt Lillie, your girlfriend or your neighbor. What works for them may not work for you. I am now speaking about strategies, not principles.

Principles work for everyone, but strategies vary depending on people, places and circumstances. Every child is different with different personalities and gifts. They can be born of the same two parents and be different as night and day. Can I get a witness?

Sometimes in trying to take care of all the physical needs of a child, we miss out on some of those really intimate times of connection. We capture some, and others are amidst. All of my kids are grown, and I can't honestly say that I captured every intimate moment. Here is what I want you to know. Being a purposeful parent doesn't mean you are a perfect one.

Parenting under any circumstance is a challenge. Not an easy job. But single parenting can be downright exhausting physically and emotionally. Can I get a witness?

If you have never been a single parent, you have no idea. Yeah, people know that it is different from having both parents share in the load, but they have no idea how different. Let me see if I can paint the picture. It is like skiing with only one ski. Instead of having the support of two skis, you have to find a way to balance on one as you travel down the slopes.

It is like playing a game of basketball with no bench, but your opponent is fully stacked and benched. Let's not stop there. It is like playing baseball, and it's your turn up to bat, but you have no bat for the curveball. These all may sound extreme, but I really wanted to paint the picture of how we single parents sometimes feel. Being a single parent sometimes feels like you're walking a tightrope with no safety net. Exactly! If you are fortunate, you may have some type of help sometime.

There were times in my journey I did get help, random acts of kindness from a friend or relative. My kid's grandmother stepped in at strategic times in their high school senior year and college.

I am truly thankful for any help that I received. But I have to say, even with that help, I struggled to keep the homestead afloat while contributing to all my son's future, even with help. That is to say to the single parent, the higher you reach, the harder the struggle. The more children you have, usually the tougher the road. At the end of the day, you, the single parent, have to be the standup guy or girl. I talk about being that hero, but the truth is that we don't live in a perfect world that gives us perfect situations. We don't walk out of the house or live in it as perfect people. Perfection is not a reality. Earlier, I mentioned how even though we can never be perfect, we can strive to be exceptional, outstanding, priceless, skillful, good, admirable and wonderful.

All of these things are great, but none of them mean perfect. Reflecting on my own journey as a single parent, there were those who looked at me and my life in raising my three sons and gave me all kinds of accolades. Some have said, "You are a strong woman," or "I thought you were superwoman," or "you have done a great job." No one has ever said, "You have done perfectly," because I hadn't. I didn't always do the right thing at the right time. We as people are flawed, and as single parents, we are raising flawed people all while trying to charter a flawed system.

In writing this book, I am speaking to the REAL. Real people with real life, everyday challenges. Let me see if I can clear it up for you. Have you ever saw a movie where there was a national disaster or devastating storms. Folks had to make life and death decisions because help could not get to them when the storm first broke out. So they had to devise a plan as they went.

Ok, right here, I am giving you a peek into the chapter to follow but what I mean is that as a single parent, if help comes later or never comes, you are it. You are the help. So whether you feel like it or not, you have to find the strength to get it done. Somehow, someway, someday. Remember, all days are not the same.

You will have those near-perfect days. Those days where you need to pinch yourself because everything pretty much went as planned. Then you will have those days where you don't know what to do because nothing seemed to go right. These are the days when you just give everything to the Father and shout, "Jesus take the wheel."

The reality of it all is that single parenthood is tough. Imagine already being financially stretched, dealing with everyday issues and decisions you have to make. We all have our life challenges, tragedies, near tragedies, disappointments, let downs and the list goes on. Think about going at it alone.

It's even more difficult. It is like playing doubles at a tennis tournament, and you're the only one on your side of the net trying to defend the team. Reality Check. You don't have to go at it alone. God is right there, just waiting for you to ask him to take the lead. Your thinking, yeah, right.

I am well aware that everything in the sense of the word tells you that you are alone. You feel alone, carry pain alone, struggle to make ends meet alone, plan alone, cry alone, and sometimes even laugh alone. You can even have someone special in your life or someone who helps here and there, but you still carry the brunt of it all.

When God leads, he takes the effect of the brunt and softens it. He softens the brunt of being in a hard place. In the midst of all that goes on in your life, he is right there. Even when it seems as if you're talking and he is not listening. When you get to the end of yourself, he is right there.

There were many times when I was at the end of myself. And then he carried me. Wow! Just thinking about it tears me up because this is my truth. There are those who will and can take many things away from you if you allow, but no one can take away what you know to be your truth.

In It to Win It
Chapter 2 Reflections
'the reality of It all'

When was the moment you decided that your family was going to win no matter the obstacles you faced?

(e.g., when you first found out you were becoming a single parent, when you accomplished some goals in spite of your circumstance)

1._____

2._____

3._____

4._____

What plans do you have in place which will help you overcome the stigma and challenges of single parenthood?

(e.g., start or go back to school, create a budget)

1._____

2._____

3._____

4._____

Been There Done That

Has your vision for your family changed now that it is being led by one parent instead of two? If so, how?

(e.g., it is smaller, it is bigger)

1._____

2._____

3._____

4._____

CHAPTER THREE

No Plan, It's Ok

*W*ouldn't it be great if kids came with an instructional manual or if life itself came with a playbook? Unfortunately, that is not the case. When I became a single parent, I had no idea of what I was in for. All I knew was that my kids needed me, and I had to be there because no one else was. I had no plan and no strategy for making things work.

No outstanding examples of how things should go and what they should be. I just knew it had to happen, and to make it happen, I had to make the right decisions most of the time at the most important times. Even if those right decisions meant that I came in last or did without so that my children could have what they needed.

I began to take one day at a time and put one foot in front of the other. I didn't have a plan, but that was ok because God did. Just because your plan A didn't work out, it doesn't mean that your plan B or C will not lead you straight into the direct path of God's plan A for your life.

Jeremiah 29:11

For I know the thoughts and plans that I have for you, says the Lord, thoughts and plans for welfare and peace and not for evil, to give you hope in your final outcome.

So now your resume reads single parent. What's next? To be honest, you may not know what comes next. In that case, turn to the experts. Who are the experts? I am glad you asked. I know of three of them who can counsel you in every situation.

They will show you what to do with every attitude and disposition you will encounter while raising your kids. They have done it all, seen it all and don't mind sharing. Who am I talking about? The Trinity. No, I am not getting all spiritual on you, but this is my truth. I am just sharing how I kept my sanity while single parenting. In raising children, you have to learn how to work with different temperaments and dispositions. You have to learn what makes them tick, what makes them happy, what makes that smile, what makes them cry. You learn their insecurities, strengths, fears, hopes, dreams, likes, and dislikes.

I surely did not master all of these but the ones I did, allowed me to be instrumental in shaping their future. I knew the creator of the universe had to have all the answers because he made everything and everybody. Therefore it just made sense to me to include him in the rearing of the next generation. I didn't know a lot, but I knew I wanted to lay a firm foundation when it came to their belief system.

My experiences in life taught me that they, too, would have some disappointments, some not-so-good days, some temptations, some peer pressure and some discouragement layered on top of all that foundation.

A house is only as strong as the foundation it is built on. So as people, we are only as strong as the foundational teachings that we were raised on.

When you find yourself in a situation with no plan and your back is against the wall, just know that God has a plan. His plan for you existed before the very foundations of the earth. So you having no plan is no excuse not to walk out things in excellence.

Walking single parenthood out in excellence is not winging it or guesstimating. Not sure if these are words but there, I said it. You don't have to walk around guessing about what you need to do all the time. Need not it be said, yes, there were many times I had no idea what to do.

If you trust him, he will lead you. God, that is. Nothing takes him by surprise. Right about here, you are probably thinking, so why did he let this happen to me. News flash! We do make our own decisions that carry consequences. When I was faced with raising these boys alone, I didn't follow a twelve-point plan or consult with a psychologist with a PhD. These all would have been a great help, I am sure. I am just saying that this was not my reality.

For me, I knew I would need help outside of myself if I was to be a positive impact in the lives of my children at any age. I knew if I was going to survive my newfound life, I would need supernatural intervention. Remember those "Out of the gate years."

We, as parents, only have a short time to pour into our kids' lives as the Chief Influencer. To tell the truth, you don't even get all of that time before other people, places and things start to compete and pound upon the core values and foundation you have built for your children to stand on.

I didn't have a plan, but I did develop a strategy. Instead of having total meltdowns when frustrated, I developed a prayer life. I meditated on good even if I felt bad. This was my strategy most of the time. I said most of the time because there were times of meltdowns. I had days of "Today is my pity party day, and I will start anew tomorrow, but right now, I am in my feelings."

Single parents, especially single moms, are usually looked down upon. Society looks at single parenthood as extra baggage that stops you from achieving your dreams or stops you from enjoying life. I understand their view. Statistics are all stacked against us. It is downright scary and discouraging to read them. Many of us believe in what they tell us.

The overall message that the statistics of a single parent voices is that you might as well give up and let it be. Accept the report, what will be will be. Question? Who said it had to be that way for you and your children?

What authority do they have over you and your family life and destiny? Answer. Only what you give them. So don't just take things as they seem when you and your children's lives hang in the balance.

Decisions, decisions, decisions. What report are you going to believe? The world statistical view or God's statistical view? Now the statistics on single parenting are all facts but don't have to be for you. They do not have to be your truth.

Been There Done That

Do you give up and accept the norm. Do you accept the doom and gloom, or do you stand up with all the strength you have and overcome the odds? How about believing what God said about your condition and future.

The one thing I do know is that prayer changes things. Let me say that again with a shout. Prayer changes things! Now let me be more practical. Prayer plus execution changes things. When you pray, God will give you instructions to do something and how to get it done. Looking back over my life, I can see where situations and circumstances changed. Did they change immediately? No, not for me. There were lessons to be learned, so I had to be processed. Are there still challenges and struggles, of course? As long as you live, there will be. But they should not be the same struggles.

I now look back and realize the hand of God over my life, and I am in awe. He is faithful. While I thought I would lose it because I could not see my way, he had already made the way. He preserved me through all the throwing of the lemons until it was time to make sweet lemonade. God held me close through it all.

I can truly say everything good and grand that has happened in my life. God did it! There were many times I had no idea of how I was going to make it or how things were going to turn out. Single parenthood was too big for me to handle alone.

As a single parent, you have to provide all that is needed somehow, someway. You have to make all the decisions, whether they turn out to be good or bad. You have to juggle your kid's schedule along with your schedule.

You have to play the role of a Therapist even when there are days you feel as if you could use a little therapy yourself. You have to comfort and support even when you are the one who needs comforting and supporting.

In providing as a single parent, you have to try and make ends meet that never meets. You have to make sure that the kids are balanced even when you feel off balance. This is the truth and nothing but the truth. I mean, come on, it takes Superman, Superwoman, Spider-Man, Batman, Robin and the Black Panther to accomplish all of this perfectly, and God knew I was no superhero and perfection wasn't going to happen on my time clock.

There were times when I found myself saying to God, "Really, are you serious." I am not a superhero. I need rescuing myself.

Been There Done That

Now what
Chapter 3 Reflections
'No plan, It's Ok'

What practical choices can you put into place to guide your family in living as a victor and not the victim?

(e.g., prayer, family meetings)

1._____

2._____

3._____

4._____

How does focusing on the future motivate you to stay positive?

(e.g., promotes creative thinking, gives you hope)

1._____

2._____

3._____

4._____

Been There Done That

Choosing to win has to be intentional. How does choosing to win look like when it seems as if you are in a losing situation?

(e.g., unattainable, just another challenge)

1._____

2._____

3._____

4._____

CHAPTER FOUR

Pick Your Battles

A battle is a hostile encounter or engagement between opposing military forces. It's a contest, conflict, war. It is any conflict or struggle. If you are battling, then you are struggling or striving toward something or some goal.

Single parenthood can be exhausting, and this is why you have to learn how to pick your battles. Not everything should lead to World War III. This is where wisdom comes in and your ability to allow the Holy Spirit to guide and teach you. Usually, when we try and solve problems our way, we create an even bigger problem. We make even a bigger mess of things. We start to try and solve them out of our own intellect and experiences.

Been There Done That

If we knew the future, then this would be great. All problems solved. Only if it was that simple. The truth is that we don't know the future. We don't even know if tomorrow will come—our wit and know-how will only take us thus far. So in knowing this, I chose to lean and depend on God. That is most of the time. There were times when I thought to myself that I could not wait on God. He was taking too long. Have you ever felt that way?

There were times when I would think to myself, "God, what are you waiting on? Can't you see me about to pass out over here? "Can you just give me the ok to handle this situation my way? Can you allow me to just get it out, say what's on my mind because they sure do deserve it? You know how we get when we want to so-called give someone a piece of our mind. You may be asking yourself, "How do I choose my battles."

There are so many, and all seem to be important. All of them are important, but all of them are not equally important. It is important that you teach lessons where discipline and principles are a priority. Still, there are times when the bigger picture is love, tolerance, etc.

How do we know what battles to fight?

We don't always? We sometimes find ourselves fighting to no end about things that will work themselves out if we would just get out of the way. Picking your battles just means that you are not swinging aimlessly at everything that upsets up or ticks you off.

Now I know that I am throwing the phrase around, "picking your battles to fight," but as believers, we know that our fight is spiritual and not physical. That ultimately the battle is the Lords. What I mean is that we must have a sense of what situations need our attention and which ones are just mere distractions.

Being a single parent means that you have to strategize your success. Yes, I did say success. Raising kids by yourself and surviving it with excellence is being successful. I know what you are saying. By the world standard, success is everything but that. Well, you have to ask yourself what standard you're following. Remember, your children's destiny is at stake. Their call and purpose hang in the balance. You are a chief influencer in their lives. You're modeling and shaping the next generation. I don't know about you, but when I look at CNN and the local news and just the world culture as we see it, I am sometimes floored.

Sometimes, I think that if I did not raise my kids with Godly standards, then where would they be? Mind you, they are far from perfect and have made their share of mistakes, but I think to myself, how much imbedded they would be in the worldly culture if I hadn't. Let me be clear. I am not saying they don't believe in the culture because they do. However, I just cannot help but think that they might have gotten caught up in things that would have taken them in the wrong direction further than they wanted to go, deeper than they expected.

This life is full of choices. Choices to thrive, to live, or you can choose to give up. You can choose to allow others to define you. You can choose to live on your own terms. You can choose hope. You can choose to dream. You can choose to get up if you've been down. You can choose to sow good deeds or to sow bad ones. There is a shipload of choices in life, and we get to choose.

This brings us to battle choices. If the United States of America entered into every conflict they thought had an interest to us, then we would deplete our military and resources. This is why they have to strategically assess the pros and cons of going to war. Now, as single parents, we may not be going to physical war, but we do war. Our ultimate battle is the battle of raising balanced, self-reliant, loving adults. In trying to do this, we have to ensure that we do not get sidetracked in pettiness.

Pettiness means that you are majoring in the minors. Majoring in things that, at the end of the day, do not carry any weight. So what if they do not like you, like your hair or the clothes you wear? So what if your name is famous in the mouths of others and they cannot stand to see you coming? So what if your kids are not perfect and others cannot see their destiny or future? So what? So what if your sacrifice seems to make you look as if your status is on skid row?

So what? People talk!

Let them. This is not your battle. Let things fall where they may. Those who are truly a part of your destiny will be there and encourage you to go farther.

Let go of the baggage that keeps trying to attach itself to you. Remember, the enemy has a strategy too. His strategy is to keep you distracted with the small stuff that appears huge in your life so that you never walk in the purpose and your calling God has predestined for your life. Keep moving.

How do you keep moving?

You keep moving swiftly with minimal baggage. We all have baggage, and some of it never goes away. However, we can learn how to overcome it by putting it to the side and moving past it, It won't be that it is not a part of who you are, but it will not be who you are. Your pass baggage does not have to control your life. Don't carry it, don't put it in a bag, wheel it or drag it, and lose it.

So anything that so easily beset you, shake it off. My old pastor, Marvin M.L. Anderson, used to always say, "Shake the devil off." And that is exactly what you have to do. Move swiftly and shake him off. Shake him off with prayer, praise and perseverance. Shake him off with love, longsuffering and kindness. Shake him off with the knowledge of Christ and his word.

It is like being in a race. You come out of the blocks in your lane, and your focus is on the finish line. The enemy wants you to stay loaded down with things you cannot change. No one can change their past; however, the past hunts many of us and cause us to fear the future.

When you are racing, you don't wave to the people on the sidelines. This is a distraction. This will cause you to trip (start tripping), fall (fall down), or just slow down (slow your progress). Fighting the wrong battle will have you all over the place. In order to overcome all distractions, you must develop what is called tunnel vision. Tunnel vision is having a drastically narrowed field of vision, as looking through an actual tunnel. Everything you do must line up with where you want to go, which is to make it to the finish line with your sanity and stronger than ever.

Stay focused.

See, when you lose focus, you begin to allow other people to pull you into their web and what they have going on. You allow others to pull you into their world. You know, gossip, mess, negative talk, stinking thinking and so forth. Here is where choices come into play. You have to ask yourself, "Who am I, what do I believe and where do I want my family to go."

You have to ask yourself will this help or hinder me, my children or my family. Your answer will tell you if the battle is worth the fight. Now there will be times that you must fight. Spiritually that is. I have had to spiritually fight just to stay on course. There is a time to fight and a time to just give things a nod because they are just not worth your time. Remember, there is a time for everything under the sun.

A Time for Everything
1 For everything there is a season,
A time for every activity under heaven.
2 A time to be born and a time to die.
A time to plant and a time to harvest.
3 A time to kill and a time to heal.
A time to tear down and a time to build up.
4 A time to cry and a time to laugh.
A time to grieve and a time to dance.
5 A time to scatter stones and a time to gather stones.
A time to embrace and a time to turn away.
6 A time to search and a time to quit searching.

Been There Done That

A time to keep and a time to throw away.
7 A time to tear and a time to mend.
A time to be quiet and a time to speak.
8 A time to love and a time to hate.
A time for war and a time for peace.

Ecclesiastes 3:1

As single parents, our time is extremely important because there are so many things that contend for it. Finding time for yourself is little or of no existence. So we must examine everything that bids for our time and attention. This is why we must pick our battles carefully because some things are just not worth our time. That is if you are trying to do this thing with excellence.

Now, if you are just getting through the day and letting the chips fall where they may when it comes to raising your kids, then so be it. However, if you are in tune with the destiny of the next generation and your responsibility in helping to guide them to where they need to be, then you do not have time for foolishness.

You must overcome the distractions. You know those sideline conversations and endeavors. This does not mean that you do not stop to smell the roses or enjoy the sunshine. What it means is you have to have balance in all that you do.

Everybody has their down days, the "I'm just taking a day," and their days to refresh for the next fight. I am not talking about that. I mean that you do not have time to wallow in things that suck up all of your energy and do not empower you.

You do not have time to major in the minor. Even King David chose his battles. There were times that he stood for the battle, and other times he ran toward his destiny, leaving the battle behind. Every day has its troubles, struggles and disappointments, so choose well.

You don't have to show up to every argument you're invited to. There is only a limited amount of time between the dashes. You know, the one that will be placed on your tombstone with the day you were born and the day you expirer. Think about. I am saying think about it, but most people spend their whole lives finding ways not to give it no thought.

One way to effectively choose your battles is to look at the big picture with discernment. For example, if you are dealing with a child who has a behavioral problem, instead of trying to deal with every aspect of the child's behavior, the parent could pick the most serious issue to focus on first, like the tendency to stay out past curfew. There is always a root cause, so finding out the root cause in any problem is key.

Once this issue is dealt with, the parent can move on to other problems. If the main problem, or shall I say the root of the problem, is dealt with successfully, it will sometimes help the other underlining hindrances. You see how focusing on what's most important can most times help resolve all those other small problems that we saw as giants when, in fact, they were nothing but grasshoppers.

I found that when a giant of a problem arose, the word of God was faithful. The word of God is time-tested. That means it worked time and time again. It is not what someone else said they did in their situation and try to fit your situation in the same scope. The word of God is true and unfailing when all else around you is tumbling down.

God will do this, for he is faithful to do what he says, and he has invited you into partnership with his Son, Jesus Christ our Lord.

I Corinthians 1:9

God is faithful [He is reliable, trustworthy and ever true to His promise—He can be depended on], and through Him you were called into fellowship with His Son, Jesus Christ our Lord.

When needing answers to solve life's problems, why would you not go to the source that created life—God? Is it that you don't believe that he is who he says he is? Or that his way of doing things does not interest you because he takes too long to get things done? Or that His way always seems to take the scenic route, you know, like your GPS?

You think to yourself, I know that there is a shorter route because you kind of know the area. However, the GPS gives you the route of its preference to get you to where you are going. Now mind you, I feel the same way at times with my GPS. I am like, now I know the area, and this GPS is taking me out the way. And sometimes I am right.

The man-made device will do just that. But when the word of God is your GPS, it is always on point, even when it seems as if it is taking you the scenic route.

So amid the battle, just be assured that the author and finisher of your faith will bring you through the journey and will get you to your destination on time.

One of the main reasons to carefully pick your battles is that you need to save your strength for the war. Not saying that all things are not important. Again they are not as equally important. Here is where you need to know what season you're in. Knowing the season you're in will help you prioritize things, size things up and keep them in order of importance. Otherwise, you will be all over the place.

Your thoughts will be consumed. The pressure of seeming like you're always in a fight will overtake you. Operating out of season will frustrate you. Here is where knowing how to fight spiritually really comes into play.

Spiritual warfare is key to overcoming any obstacle or adversity. Being an overcomer requires knowledge of the word of God and the willingness to submit and a sense of the season you're in. Ok, you may say that knowing your season is not that difficult. You are a single parent and your season is raising and providing for these kids you have.

You are in a season of raising up and preparing the next generation. This is you, single parent.

Knowing your season is half the battle. The other half is trusting God through the season of life you are in.

Listen to the promise for you that comes straight from the heart of Father God:

Romans 15:13

May the God of hope fill you with all joy and peace as you trust in him.

So that you may overflow with hope by the power of the Holy Spirit.

Did you hear it? Joy, peace and hope offered to you by the God of hope!! This is not just a promise to "get by" or to be a "survivor" – it's a promise of overflowing with hope – of being filled with joy and peace!!

Every season comes with its ups and downs, its joys and troubles. I don't know about you, but I do not want to spend not one season in a down, depressed state of mind. The enemy wants to steal your joy, your hope and definitely your future.

As single parents, you have so much that will come up against you and your purpose that you will have many times when you will just want to throw in the towel. Your trust is not in your ability, but God's ability to handle your situation will determine how and if you will survive single parenthood with your sanity.

Zechariah 4:6

So he said to me, "This is the word of the LORD to Zerubbabel: 'Not by might nor by power, but by my Spirit,' says the LORD Almighty.

This is how you and your family will overcome the Adversary. It will not be by your own power. Not your name, who you know, your degrees, your relationship or your money. It will be by God's spirit.

How do you get there?

Been There Done That

You must get to that position of submission, which will allow God to move by his spirit in your circumstance and give you the victory. In the case of all parents, especially single parents, there will be many battles to fight, so you will need victories (plural).

Making the right Choices
Chapter 4 Reflections
'Pick Your Battles'

What battles are you facing at the moment and what battles do you need to let go of?

(e.g., relationship, financial)

1._____

2._____

3._____

4._____

How will you choose between what situations are merely a distraction and what situations truly warrant your attention?

(e.g., impacts future, impacts family)

1._____

2._____

3._____

4._____

Been There Done That

How does picking the right battles to fight help you eliminate distractions?

(e.g., keeps you on track, avoid wasting time)

1._____

2._____

3._____

4._____

CHAPTER FIVE

Calling Forth Greatness

*J*esus Christ, the Master, was the master in calling forth the great which was in individuals. He called forth greatness in all of his disciples, who all struggled with walking in their calling even though they walked right along with him.

When we think of someone great, we think of them doing great things or being larger than life. Jesus called many out of the situations they were born in. Many of us find ourselves in circumstances that are not a part of our destiny.

For example, when he healed the lame man, he commanded him to pick up his bed and walk. The blind man he commanded him to see. He was calling them out of everything that life had dealt them. Not to mention the disciples who he called out of their mundane, run-of-the-mill, everyday job to follow him, which also translated into doing something new.

So if life has dealt you a single-parent home, you can be called out of the effects of its residue. You can overcome any of its obstacles.

In a single-parent home, no matter how much that child is loved and cared for, they can still grow up with issues and residue from not having the completeness of a loving two-parent home. Notice I emphasized loving. Whether it's not having what the Joneses have or not having the time spent with them because a parent has to work all the time to make ends meet.

In my case, it was all the above. It was missing that father figure and that mom having to fill in where she could. I just could not only play that loving savior of a mother, but I had to also be the disciplinary that showed tough love.

The void for boys not having a father in the home runs deeper than we know. However, your words have power. That is what calling forth greatness is. It's reaching into someone's lot in life and saying, "I don't care what it looks like, where you came from, or what you have been through, you are significant, and I'm going to help you see that. Jesus made people noteworthy, meaningful, extraordinary, exceptional, and special.

He knew that God had a purpose in them as part of his story. When the smoke clears and all the battle lines have been drawn, we are all just a part of his story to bring about his purpose. Now that is significant.

God, the creator, has cast you to play a part in his story. Wow, now that is important. News flash! He is still writing his story to include you and your children. Even though statistics tell us that 70 percent of men that are incarcerated are from fatherless homes. Yes, the statistics for single-parent homes are ugly and discouraging, but God.

Growing up in the church, I always heard folks say, Jesus makes the difference. As I began to experience life, I realize that this actually was true. He makes all the difference. It rains on the just as well as the unjust, but the just have Jesus for real, and that makes the difference. I can truly say that I would have fainted, quit and threw in the towel without him. When the storms of life come, and oh they will come, they have no respect of person, make sure your anchor holds. Jesus is the anchor.

The headline of my life reads, "Without him, I would have fainted."

"With him, I almost fainted." There were times when I was out on the brink of giving up, even with him. I know that some of you, who haven't really experienced much, might say, "How can I say that I almost gave up when I was supposed to be trusting in Jesus.

For with him, you should be strong at all times, courageous at all times and having it all together at all times." I hear you loud and clear. I understand why you would ask that question.

Let me answer you like this. Once you have experienced life trials and truly experienced being more than a conqueror, then you will get it. Anyone can be a conqueror in a given situation, but to be more than signifies that God was glorified through the turbulence. Let's look at this a little closer.

When parents call forth greatness in their children, they are calling forth that which is not developed or has been tapped into. They can look at a child, whether that child is unmotivated, troubled, or a well-rounded kid and begin to speak into them what God has ordained them to speak.

There were many times that I would mimic the Jewish custom in the laying of the hands on their children. I did this many times, commanding the blessing over their lives.

There was no father in the home for the most part, so I was it. I just believed in faith that it would make a difference. No one knows the ending to their story, but you can know that because you allow God to write the script, everything will be alright for you and your kids. Why? Because it is already written.

Jacob is a great example of what God can do. Jacob came from a lineage of con artists, liars and tricksters. He wanted what he wanted. He did not care who he had to take down to get it. It was in his bloodline. You may already know the story.

He stole his brother's birthright with the help of his mother. His uncle Laban was a trickster. It was in the bloodline. God would later call forth greatness in him. He is to this day still considered to be a patriarch of the Israelites.

There is an artwork on the campus of Abilene Christian University, which is known as 'Jacobs Dream Statue.'

Now, this is good for someone who started out as a trickster. Another example of God calling forth greatness was in King David. David always lived in the shadow of his brothers. He was overlooked by people and was never front and center. You know he was never the favorite until God interrupted his destiny and anointed him King.

God has the power to call forth greatness, and since we are made in his image, so do we. Greatness is in every one of us. It just needs to be pulled out of most of us.

Jacob and David did not have a life served on a silver platter. So your circumstance with your kids may not be ideal, but there is good news. The word of God is good news, and it gives us instruction on how to speak those things that be not as though they were.

Does speaking your hopes and dreams negate the fact you have to work hard for it? Absolutely not!

I do not know about you, but even though you work hard at something, it is just good to know God is in your corner.

Children react to what they see and hear. If they hear that they are no good and can't do anything, that is what they will believe. If life is spoken into their lives, they will live. If it is not, they will just exist as a shell of other people's opinions.

Parents have to ask themselves, "What type of environment are you creating for your kids. It is great to live in a big house, in the right neighborhood with all the toys imaginable. Nothing is wrong with that in itself. But this is not the reality for most.

When I mention the environment here, it is speaking to whether the home environment is hostile or peaceful. Is home a safe haven mentally and physically for your children.

I tried to set a relaxed atmosphere in the home—a place where they could feel received and loved no matter what's going on around them. They need to feel they were loved. Love is the key. When a child feels loved, they can do anything.

Home is where a child gets watered so that they can flourish out in the world. A child is a seed, and how you water them is with love, assurance, and courage to face the world.

As a single parent, our situation was not great. Most times, they were tough, even when it looked easy. That was just the grace of it all. Your circumstances may not be ideal, but you can choose to create an environment full of love. Love will save the day.

I never had a lot of material things to give my kids outside of the basics and the necessities. There never was an overflow of things, but there was an overflow of love. Love was there, concern was there, peace was there, hope for the future was there and an avenue to dream was there.

When this is the case, a child can thrive no matter what else is lacking. If there are any behavioral or self-confidence issues, they will not stop greatness from showing up. Love saves the day, the week, the month, the year and destinies.

Of course, there are times when love is there, but it is rejected. This does happen because you are not your child's only influence. But as a parent, your part is to do your part. Be the parent. Be the difference because remember you are the chief influencer.

Been There Done That

Every child is different. Some are go-getters, while some move about as turtles. Some are kind and loving, while others may be stubborn and self-centered. Some are super smart and quick to learn. While others may be struggling just to keep up.

No matter how that child has been wired, each has the strongest desire to be loved, respected and accepted. As parents, we owe them that because guess what? You got it; they did not ask to be here. Calling forth greatness doesn't mean that their greatness is being an NBA superstar, an NFL quarterback or the president of a country. If this is their lot, then wonderful.

Calling forth greatness is simply calling forth that in a child that helps them understand that they are special and that thing which makes them special should shine.

In spite of all their shortcomings and struggles quitting is not an option. Not for the parent or the child. You're in it to win it. Raising kids is about building people—little people. Whatever that child lacks, it is up to the parent to make up what they can and leave the rest to God.

That is as much as they can, and the rest, the child just put it in God's hand. As single parents, we must keep in mind that we're no perfect, and we don't have all the answers.

Say It Ain't So

As single parents, you have to know that all that you can't do, God can. When you wake up every day knowing this, you can walk in excellence. You can walk with your head up no matter what the devil throws at you. Allow God to regulate your relationship with your children.

Growing up, I did not get the sacrifice of my grandmother, who raised me till I was 12, or my mother, who worked tirelessly at a local hospital.

I didn't know the cost, but now I do. So, parents, know that your children may not fully get it. They may not fully get your sacrifice until they are much older and have experienced some things and have children of their own.

Been There Done That

Destined
Chapter 5 Reflections
'Calling Forth Greatness'

How would you describe the greatness within? Is it simply being significant?

(e.g., serving others with your gift, making a difference)

1._____

2._____

3._____

4._____

How are you going to help guide and develop that greatness within your children?

(e.g., affirmations, education, scripture)

1._____

2._____

3._____

4._____

Been There Done That

Why do you believe as a parent you are responsible for help developing the gift within them?

(e.g., righteous duty, accountability)

1._____

2._____

3._____

4._____

CHAPTER SIX

Don't Panic in the Pain

Isaiah 66:9

I will not cause pain without something new to be born.

Psalms 147:3

He heals the broken-hearted and binds up their wounds.

No one wants to be inconvenienced or feel pain. Pain is a distressing feeling often caused by intense or damaging stimuli. As a single parent, you may have been in a situation that caused you pain which may have led you into single parenthood.

Whatever the pain was or where it came from or how it came, don't panic. There was a very popular song out when I was coming up. Some of you may remember it.' No pain, No gain.' The point of the message is that in life, real growth comes from painful experiences.

I will be the first to say that some experiences can and should be avoided. However, life has a way of making sure that you understand that a bed of roses is not guaranteed, and if by chance you lay in them for one season, there is no guarantee it will be roses the next.

But don't panic.

As a single parent, I had to learn to take one day at a time. Meaning I had to take each day as it came. When things did not go right and my back was against the wall, I had to walk that thing out.

I could not afford to have a meltdown when it came to making decisions that would affect my family. Whether all the decisions were great, that is still on the table. What I can tell you is that not panicking allowed me to move forward and not be consumed in the pain.

Your pain may be a loss of a loved one, abuse, ill words spoke against you, rejection, failure or any other negative action that came against you. I agree that there are different levels of pain, but pain is pain at the end of the day. It is unwanted. Whoever says, "Bring on all the pain"?

So here you are, a single parent facing one of the greatest challenges of your life. I know some people just go through the motions half-heartedly as a 'must do' instead of an 'I get to do.'

There goes perspective again.

How you see your pain will determine if you will panic when it looks like your world is falling all apart around you. The person who is not in panic will say, "All around me is sinking, but I am soaring." No matter what you see with the natural eye, your eye of faith causes you to soar even in the face of failed situations.

Looking at things with my natural eyes, I was a single parent with three small kids with limited funds and limited resources. I knew the statistics and the picture it painted for single parents and their children. I could have panicked and began to trust in things that would have led me away from the purpose God had for me. My purpose to be used as an instrument to inspire, encourage and empower other single parents to do the same. Panic leads you away from your purpose. Panic takes your focus off what God has for you. It tells you that your circumstances will never change and that panicking will make the difference.

I beg to differ. The devil is a liar. Panic only brings on more panic. So don't panic. Panic is a byproduct of fear. Fear (false evidence appearing real).

False:

False Evidence Appearing Real Not real, Not Truth

II Timothy 1:7

For God has not given us the spirit of fear but of power, love and a sound mind.

In order to overcome fear, you first must know who you are. In order to know that, you have to know whose you are. "Fear not "is in the Bible 365 times. One for every day of the year. Isn't that amazing? Look at God. He knew we would need to be encouraged every day to overcome fear.

Evidence: The available body of facts or information indicating whether a belief or proposition is true or valid.

Hebrews 11:1

Now faith is the assurance of things hope for, being the proof of things we do not see and the conviction of their reality.

In a court of law, evidence covers the burden of proof. Evidence is the proof of what is trying to be proven. If a prosecutor is trying to convict a person, he needs evidence to help him do so.

As single parents, we want that evidence that shows that we have victory in life in raising our kids while being kept ourselves. Fear shows us evidence of things that paralyze us in our steps. It pushes us into that panic mode. We become frazzled and lose our focus and courage to be our best selves.

Our best selves is being ourselves and living out our God-given purpose while maturing the foundational purposes of our children through prayer, love, and being intentional.

Appearing: To come into sight; become visible or noticeable, seem, give the impression or being.

Romans 8:37

Yet amid all these things, we are more than conquerors and gain a surpassing victory through Him Who loved us.

While navigating the waters of single parenthood, there were many times when things appeared hopeless, as if nothing would ever change. There were times when I felt defeated, and thoughts would cross my mind like, 'what's the use.' There were times when I just wanted to lose focus on purpose and just do me, whatever that means.

The pressures of single parenting, along with the world outlook of those affected by it and its weight, will sometimes make you want to throw up your hands and quit. Quit what? I am glad you asked.

Quit going the extra mile to show your children that with God, anything is possible. It appeared to some that my situation was hopeless, if not just mediocre. It appeared that with all that was stacked against me as a single parent, especially a poor one, the negative would happen. People expect the negative in you and your children's life because they just cannot see past what appears to be the norm.

Real: actually existing or happening: not imaginary: not fake, or artificial.

Isaiah 40:8

The grass withers, the flower fades, but the word of our God will stand forever.

Here is why it is dangerous to measure everything by how you feel. Feelings change. People, places and things can change. Nothing is constant but the word of God.

Check your history. The real is what it says about your ability to walk out of your state of single parenthood.

Above what seems real, above what you know to be the facts? Above what is being whispered and what others are saying. Above the battlefield of the mind.

I am a witness that it will see you through, guide you through and take you through to the other side. The other side of single parenthood where you can see the fruit of your labor. Now that's real. I am a testimony of what he can and will do even in the face of adversity. Real as real can be.

Do not panic in your pain. Pain goes away. Try to remember the last time you stomped your toe. Can you still feel the pain? Probably not. Now I did say pain goes away, but I am aware that some types of pain never really fully go away. However, as overcomers, we learn how to function and excel through it.

As single parents, we must push through any past pain to move forward and move our children forward toward their destiny. So don't panic, push. Push through the disappointments, negativity, failures, the expectations of others and your own fears and doubts. Push! Push! Push!

Been There Done That

We are More than Conquerors
Chapter 6 Reflections
'Don't panic in the pain'

Describe a specific pain in your life you are dealing with or have overcome?

(e.g., loss, health)

1._____

2._____

3._____

4._____

What has the pain you have experienced taught you about life?

(e.g., it passes, it strengthens)

1._____

2._____

3._____

4._____

Been There Done That

How do you plan to use your pain for purpose?
(e.g., share it, help others)

1._____

2._____

3._____

4._____

CHAPTER SEVEN

Loving when You Need Love the Most

*A*s I searched for a quote to explain the title of this chapter, I couldn't find one that would perfectly fit it. So as I was looking, one came to mind.

> *It takes divine strength to have the capacity to love others when your love has been violated*

When you become a single parent, you quickly learn that your needs are often put on the back burner. This type of strength enables you to put yourself second and many times last only because your kids have needs. Many single parents understand exactly what this act of unselfish love requires. Let me put it this way.

Been There Done That

Financially it may require you to put off or delay getting those clothes that you desperately need for work or getting your hair done. The upside is that you become more creative. I learned how to mix and match clothes to look like a brand new outfit.

I learned creative ways to do my own hair and keep myself up without running in and out of the beauty shop making their pockets fat. Most of the money I had went toward rent, bills, kid's needs and other necessities.

Loving when you need love the most requires a heart expansion. As a single parent, you're pushed to the limits sometimes, and providing for your kids and your children's welfare is a must. Yes, there are those who place their own selfish ambitions and pleasures before everyone, including their children. They haven't yet developed the capacity to love past the pain in their lives. However, remember that the aim of this book is for parents to do their very best with what they have inside of them and with the resources they have around them.

Things are not going quite right? Do your very best. Past circumstances and generational setbacks seem like giants that won't easily go away. God has given you everything that you need to overcome any obstacle. Single parenthood has many complicated layers to it. Of course, the effect it has on most of us financially is a major layer. It just seems that there is never enough, and if somehow, one month you have more, there is always something that needs that money's attention.

Another layer of single parenthood is the emotional toll it takes on the parent. I can only share with you how I was able to put my issues on the shelf and juggle single parenthood. Not forgetting my own purpose and gifts but merely shelving them for a later date. Again if you are one who can juggle it all, by all means, do so.

I can only share with you my story and how I overcame the way that I overcame.

What got me through it was a lot of prayers—a lot of seeking the face of God on how to deal with many situations. So instead of losing my sanity, I found ways to strengthen it. Instead of believing the negative, I chose to weigh in on the positive. For me, this is what gave me the capacity to love others even when I felt that I may have needed it more.

It allowed me to still love my children even when I felt that they neglected to show that same love or simply misunderstood the love shown toward them.

No, single parenthood is not always pretty because sometimes you feel as if you give and give and never get in return. I am speaking of love, that is. As parents, we must remember that they are still growing and haven't experienced much. Just remember when we were at that stage.

Of course, when kids are young, they give you all the unconditional love you can handle. But then teen mania and the 'I love me more days begin (young adulthood).

You know the years that you ask yourself, "Whose kid is that?" Even here, love is still a requirement.

The key to surviving this stage is to not forget your blessings.

*Food in the fridge**
*Clothes in the closet**
*Bills paid for the month**
*Children needs met**

PARENTS STATE OF MIND*

Here is where you find one of the most important, if not the most important, factors in raising well-balanced kids. What a child takes in that will at some point he will display.

Something's are just in the bloodline and have to be pulled down. A parent's state of mind dictates how they will treat their children. What's deposited in a child will sit and a cure interest until it is withdrawn. No human is perfect; therefore, no child will be.

Say It Ain't So

This book is not about being a perfect parent raising perfect kids. If that is what you're looking for, good luck. But it is about empowering single parents to give it their best try.

It's about staying the course and not opting out physically or mentally. Sometimes we can be there physically, but mentally, we have checked out of the process of doing this thing with purpose.

Romans 12:2

And be not conformed to this world: but be ye transformed by the renewing of your mind that ye may prove what is good, and acceptable, and perfect, will of God.

In this age of mass technology, everything is instant, quick, at a touch and fast. Even if you don't want it, it is shoved down your throat politely, unapologetically and deceitfully.

Without you even having a chance to reject it. I am not saying technology is bad or not needed. I am saying that you have to be careful not to be consumed by all that is around you.

Your inner peace is a treasure. Nothing is more crucial. It is more important than other people's opinions of you. It is more important than your social status. It is the true you. Not the mask that everyone else sees or think they see.

Been There Done That

If keeping your emotional state in check means praying, reading a good book, taking a long hot bath, going for a massage, joining a club, writing, catching a good play, hiking, exercising, or just being around positive people, do it.

However, be very careful in trying to escape the pressures of single parenting with things that can leave you more empty and devastated in the end.

As single parents, you have to learn how to love through you. 'YOU' encompasses all that you are—the good, the bad and the ugly. You have to know that you are important too and that God has a plan for you too. You have to know that even though things in the physical haven't quite changed, that doesn't mean that they are not changing.

This chapter is titled as such because I believe single parents are special, as are all parents. However, it takes a double effort if you are a single parent. Single parents are great problem solvers. When a problem arises, they usually will find a way to solve it. If it can't be solved immediately, they will figure out a way to improvise and get by. They will manage. They learn how to do a lot with little.

Raising three kids of my own, I learned how to shop for bargains and maximize my wardrobe using the mix and match effort. When challenges popped up, and they popped up often, wisdom helped me overcome them faster so that I could move forward.

Moving forward is the key. When I look back and fast forward to now, I can see the hand of God all over the process. He was there from the beginning.

When others said no, he said YES! He said I love you dearly, and my grace is sufficient. Sufficient for you to thrive, sufficient for you to overcome, sufficient for you to get it all done.

You can love unconditionally, even when you need love the most, because God loves you unconditionally.

Been There Done That

Love Saves the Day
Chapter 7 Reflections
'Loving when You Need Love the Most'

List below the times you poured from an empty vessel?
(e.g., helping others when you were depleted, going through the motions)

1._____

2._____

3._____

4._____

How did you feel when you were empty?
(e.g., hopeless, disappointed)

1._____

2._____

3._____

4._____

Been There Done That

List below individuals you have learned to love unconditionally in your life?

(e.g., parents, friends)

1._____

2._____

3._____

4._____

CHAPTER EIGHT

Remembering the Big (P) "Purpose"

I sat and thought to myself one day, "There has to be purpose in single parenting." I mean, other than the obvious of raising kids. I know they are our future, but there has to be more. It can't be all about the children.

Yes, the children are a big part of the whole scheme of things. We as parents should be praying that God reveals his plan and purpose to our children all the time.

However, what is the purpose for you, the parent? I asked, "What is the purpose for me?"

"I know I am experiencing this for a reason, but why. I am not saying that this was God's plan or his best for me, but there has to be more."

In my heart of hearts, I didn't believe that this was it.

However, I did believe that even though the situation was less than perfect, God is still in control. God still has a destiny for the single parent. I am a living witness that he attaches purpose to a not so pleasant circumstance. There were many days when I thought, "Why are things so hard." Then I remembered there must be a purpose. God has a plan, even if I had no idea what it is.

Here is where you have to allow faith to lift you and guide you. Faith lifts you above your circumstances. It lifts you above your fear and doubt. It lifts you above all of your disappointments.

We sometimes forget God is sovereign and has written our ultimate role in life. For some of us, that is a hard pill to swallow. We all want to believe that we are in total control until we are reminded we are not. And so when things occur in our lives due to our own bad or good choices gone badly, he then fits those broken pieces of our life into a script. We are reminded again that all things work together for the good of them that loves God.

Because he has written our script, he knows how to do the editing for our good. Isn't that amazing? Wow, because God is amazing with a capital 'A.' As natural men, we would write our life script just to benefit us. God writes our life story for a purpose. If we trust God, then ultimately, our script will not just benefit us, but it will benefit our children, their children's children, and all those that you will come in contact with us. Our families would benefit, our communities would benefit, and yes, the world would benefit eternally from our reliance on God.

This is the kicker. He even lays our life script out in a way that it will even benefit people we will never meet. He sees the beginning from the ending, and the end is him being magnified.

He laces your script with hope. Hope is a powerful thing. It causes you to live to fight another day. Hope encourages you to stand in the face of adversity because we know that somewhere, deep inside, things will change.

Life happens, we make decisions, and before we know it, we are living a life that God never intended for us to live, with a mindset he did not give us. Then we look around and think, to ourselves, "How did I get here?" Let me weigh in on this.

We get there by having all the right intentions, by every decision we make or don't make. We get there by every thought we let flow through our minds and every word we allow to flow out of our mouths.

As parents, we seem to lose sight of purpose or the road to our purpose because we allow life's hustle and bustle to consume us. As for me being a single parent, survival was the name of the game. I lived to survive to the next paycheck. As a single parent, there were days I had to run around endlessly to just keep things afloat.

I mean, think about it, there is one individual who has to make sure all is well at the homestead, and everything stays going, even if it is on broken pieces.

When you add mishaps, breakdowns, and obstacles to the equation, it can be overwhelming.

Just the day-to-day grind of a single parent can be exhausting. And the more people you are responsible for makes it even more exhausting. My relief was in Him. Who? Jesus.

In him is where I found my shelter. The world can strip you of life itself if you allow it. I decided not to let it. There were and still are times when I had to go into quiet mode and hide in Him. I had to renew my mind in the word and renew my spirit daily. This was my strength.

I can almost hear some of you saying, "I have raised fine children without the aid of God." I assure you, he aided you unbeknown to you in some type of way for the greater good even if you decide not to give him the credit. He held you even if you decided not to hold on to him.

I can only testify to the power that was working in my life. I just know that I would have had to lean on something else if I was not leaning on him. So instead of making other objects, substances or ideologies my go-to, I chose God as my go-to.

Did I get it right a hundred percent of the time? You know that answer. I absolutely did not. Thank God for grace!

There is a song that my former Pastor use to sing. Here were some of the lyrics.

Have you any rivers that seem uncrossable?
And have you any mountains that you cannot tunnel through?
God specializes in things thought impossible And He will do what no other power
No other power but Holy Ghost power can do.

This was my experience. Some say experience is the best teacher, and no one can ever take away what you have experienced. No one can tell your story like you can. So when I look back now, I can see purpose in a lot of things that happened. Now mind you, there are still some things that I still don't know the purpose of and won't know till the 'Bye and Bye.'

Our lives are just not about us. It is not merely about the children we are raising or have raised. God has this big picture, and we have to play our part. You can decide not to follow his lead and do your own thing. There are consequences to our decisions.

Sometimes the part we play as single parents make us weary. Sometimes it energizes us. That's the fascinating thing about single parenting. The ride is uncertain.

'Been There, Done That, Keeping Your Sanity While Single Parenting' is meant to empower you to walk single parenthood out in excellence. Notice I did not say protection. Excellence is the quality of being outstanding or extremely good. Remember when you have done your very best, given all factors in your life, and you have exhausted all resources, then you have done excellently. Period!

The Big (P) is the purpose God has promised to fulfill in the lives of single parents if we allow him. He is a present help, and there is help in the Word of God.

The story of Hagar is a great example of a single mom that obtained the promises of God despite having to live with shame, disappointment and limited resources. God caused her to triumph over every obstacle to bring forth his promises in her life.

Genesis 21:17-19 speaks to God's provision

17 God heard the boy crying, and the angel of God called to Hagar from heaven and said to her, "What is the matter, Hagar? Do not be afraid; God has heard the boy crying as he lies there. 18 Lift the boy up and take him by the hand, for I will make him into a great nation."

19 Then God opened her eyes and she saw a well of water.

So she went and filled the skin with water and gave the boy a drink.

God will make a way out of no way. He is known for doing the impossible. Don't believe me. Check his track record.

Been There Done That

Purpose
Chapter 8 Reflections
'remembering the Big P'

What do you believe is the purpose in you being a single parent?

(e.g., to have reliance on God, to help other single parents)

1._____

2._____

3._____

4._____

List your top four priorities for your family.

(e.g., God centered, fame, status, philanthropy)

1._____

2._____

3._____

4._____

Been There Done That

What is your strategy for ensuring you and your family will live on purpose?

(e.g., implementing principles, submitting to Gods plan)

1._____

2._____

3._____

4._____

CHAPTER NINE

Let Go and Let God

God has a great plan for you and your family. We have all heard the phrase, Let Go, and let God, Especially in Christian arenas. This is one of the most difficult things for someone who is used to being in total control.

We all know that even as a single parent, you are never in total control of situations and circumstances.

Letting go means letting go of the need to be in control all of the time. Letting go of disappointments, fears, and the need to know everything. Letting go of stressing over tomorrow, which has not even come yet.

Letting go of yesterday because no matter how tight you hold on to it, you could never change. Letting go of all the things people said and say about you that was nowhere near nice.

Letting go of people who do not believe in you or who play you as small. Letting go of people who marginalize you and want you to do good but just not better than them. Letting go of others who doubted you and the God in you.

Letting go of stuff that only takes the place of being a filler in your life and does not add to your place in destiny. A life filler is all that extra stuff we do to please people and ourselves that has nothing to do with our purpose in life.

Like sitting for hours playing video games, spending hours in the presence of people who don't really care for you or your dreams. You must fight for the vision and purpose that God has destined for you. Some of us need to simply let go of some people that we are holding on to.

Letting go of past mistakes that try and cripple our present. Letting go of present circumstances that try and choke out our future. Letting go of the anxiety of the future which stops us from moving forward.

LETTING GO

If it causes you to lose focus on your dreams
Let it go

Say It Ain't So

If it hinders you from shining like a star
Let it go

If it causes you to doubt who you are
Let it go

If it leaves you feeling less than you are
Let it go

If it stops you from moving forward
Let it go

If it leaves you feeling blue
Let it go

If it leaves you feeling defeated
Let it go

If it fills you with anxiety
Let it go

If it stops you from pouring into the lives of others
Let it go

If it does not accept you for who you are
Let it go

If it doesn't have the capacity to love you like you need to be loved
Let it go

Hebrews 11:1

Now faith is the substance of things hoped for, the evidence of things not seen.

Been There Done That

As single parents, there are many hats we wear. Each and every day has its own challenges, so we do not need to carry the weight of old problems on our backs. With each day comes new obstacles, new troubles and new decisions.

Do not let the problems of yesterday through the doorway of your new day because it may cause you to lose focus on what's at hand. It may cause you to lose focus on your new goals and dreams you have for yourself and your family.

Leave your old issues where they are, in the past. Let your old problems be just that, old. Never allow your past to dictate your future.

There was a time when I allowed past hurts and pains to dictate my future. We have all been there, especially as single parents. As a single parent, I once felt that I had to carry everything in my past, which caused me to procrastinate and not move forward in my purpose.

Yes, your children should be put first when it comes to where you direct needed resources. When kids have a need, it is the parents who should fill that need. However, the more stable the parents are, the better it is for the children. This includes mental stability and financial stability.

It is difficult to maintain any sort of stability in your present state if your focus is on the past. You will not be able to clearly navigate your and your family's future. Most of all, you will not be able to hear the voice of God, which will orchestrate the navigation.

To move into the new, you must look forward towards the new things that are happening in your life and the new things which are coming.

This means you must let go of the past to move forward into your destiny.

So don't let the haters paralyze you with fear and doubt. Don't let their words heard or unheard cause you to give up on your dreams for you and your family.

You may be in a hard place as you read this right now but just know that with God, anything is impossible. You must believe that. He makes the invisible visible and the impossible possible.

Psalms 37:23

The steps of a good man are ordered by the Lord: and he delight in his way.

As a single parent, it seemed as if everything was stacked against you. I sometimes felt as if all the walls would close in on me when I began to think about all that I had to do the next day, the next week, the next month or the next year. Talk about overwhelming.

Been There Done That

It was only when I would allow Jesus to steady me that I could clearly focus on the future and the plan God had for my family and me.

Single parenthood does not have to be a life sentence. It can be that very thing that pushes you into your destiny. It will teach you many lessons, so learn from them. It offers many paths and obstacles; choose well and enjoy them all. It offers many long days and long nights, so embrace them all.

Single parenthood is what you make of it.
So make sunshine out of the rain
Lilies out of the thorns
Cotton out of the bricks
Passion out of the pain.

Your purpose may be a little difficult to figure out, but everyone knows what they are passionate about.

If you can't figure out your purpose, figure out your passion.

For your passion will lead you right into your purpose.

Then pray for revelation about what direction you are supposed to take.

It is almost impossible to walk in your purpose if your energy is spent dibbling and dabbling in the past, in old stale things, or worrying about the latest gossip about 'Who is spilling the tea on me.' Listen to this. Let it go!

As a single parent, I became passionate about empowering other single parents to want more for themselves without compromising and doing the dance of trying to live up to the expectations of others. You know that dance where you dance with people who you know do not have your best interest in mind.

You may show up to the same dance with these people, but if you are empowered and know who you are, when they begin to do their dance, you can simply say, not interested and walk away. Wow, to have that kind of power is power.

This is key. Start where you are. You may not have all your ducks in a row, and if you did, there would be no reason to trust God, right. You may not think you are where you need to be in life. We all have something we would like to change. I challenge you to use what you have and believe in God for the rest.

If you or your family are going to reach any of your goals first, you must learn to stay focused and let go of all the things that easily seat you. We get used to familiar things, even if they are the things that are hurting us or hold us back. This is what makes letting go so hard for us to do.

Been There Done That

After going through many trials and tribulations as a single parent and watching the hardships of other single parents, I became inspired to share not only my story of what inspired me but was inspired to share that encouragement that would lift another single parent up. Up out of where they now sit. Up out of that hard place.

Sometimes the hard place has nothing to do with what we have or what we do not have. Sometimes the hard place is our mindset. I wanted to give them hope of knowing that there is sunshine after the storm, which will leave a rainbow in your life. The rainbow brings new opportunities, new connections and new beginnings in your life. I can say that after each trial in my life came the sunshine.

No, things are not perfect, but things are better. Better in that I found my purpose and passion for life. It gives me energy day to day, knowing that I was put here on this earth to help others survive and thrive as a single parent.

I keep repeating that surviving does not mean everything is perfect. It does not mean that you will not have those days where you do not want to get out of bed. You will still have disagreements with your kids and issues with family stuff. It is called life.

But once you let go and let God order your steps, things become less stressful, and you learn to stop caring about other people's opinions of you. You stop putting so much time and focus into things that you cannot change. I have learned to work on the things I can change and pray about the things I can't. Simple.

Your job is the keep moving even when the road is unsure.

One step turns into two, two steps turn into three, and before you know it, you become your passion.

You begin to walk that walk of purpose. That becomes your energy bar, your energy drink and your protein shake. It energizes you when you wake up. You can't stop thinking about it when you lie down. That is passion!

Letting God lead you to how to get through a situation in the most excellent way. Most of us just want to get by on the notion that we do the best we know how to do.

When you hear someone say, "I am doing the best I can, or I did the best I could," they are speaking of doing things or what they did in their own strength. Not letting go forces you to operate in your own strength.

Letting God control the wheel allows you to operate in His power. Some things may leave you with bitterness, while other things will leave you better. Old things passed away and new things on the horizon.

So let God order your steps even in single parenthood. Don't let other folks, the world or society dictate how to raise your own children. Ask God.

Psalms 37:23

The steps of a good man are ordered by the Lord: and he delight in his way.

Some of you may ask how I let go and walk in the steps that have been ordered for me.

Where do you learn how to fight? Where do you learn how to sharpen your skills? How do you know that there is a better way? Life will teach you all of this; however, the Bible will give you the tools you need to for you and your family to be able to go forth with vision.

I use to think I would love to let God take full charge of all of my business. In my mind, I would stand back and think, "Ok, God, what are you waiting on?" That's when everything is a mess. In this chapter, I want you to understand that you need to let go and let God before things become a mess.

Life has a way of putting you into overdrive mode, and before you know it, you are back in the driver's seat with no counsel from the Wonderful Counselor himself. Just playing everything by ear. Moving and doing things as a reaction.

Say It Ain't So

You're living on the defense instead of being on the offense. We say, "Lord have your way," but do we really mean it. I beg to differ. What we speak out of our mouths is far from what is in our hearts and our minds.

So I guess you can say we have by nature a "take over spirit" when it comes to the affairs of our life. We will allow God to be the captain some of the time. We try very hard not to give up our control because we feel that we know best. Are we responsible for our own lives and those that are entrusted in our care? We are absolutely accountable! God is not going to come down here and do all our work for us.

The past always brings up our mistakes, but God, who is always present, shows us our future through his word.

Let it go!

Letting go and letting God simply means to trust the one who hued out the mountain, who set the sun in place, and who sprinkled the stars in the sky. Allow him to do what he does best, which is to orchestrate our lives from his glorious throne.

Now, if you have knowledge of the future, then, by all means, navigate your own life. God is Alpha and Omega the beginning and the ending. His words have been tried and tested. He does know the future. He created it.

The times I did not allow him to led, I found myself in an even bigger mess. I found myself in even more trouble. I found myself walking in circles, in my own wilderness.

And if I was not walking in circles, I was getting things done, but I felt very frustrated and restless. Yes, you may think you are a super mom or super dad and can accomplish things on your own. Sure. But it is so much better to do it that is single parenting with peace and resting in God.

Isaiah 32:18

My people shall dwell in a peaceable habitation, in sure dwellings, and in quiet resting places.

Letting go shows God that now you are ready to rest in him. It is doing all you can do to accomplish what needs to be done after consulting with the master and then for all the things you cannot control to rely on him to come through.

I don't care how in control you think you are; some things are just outside your reach. That is your human reach. That is if you want to be real about it. And speaking on the real, there are some things that we fear and we have anxieties about. Things that we fear that have not even happened yet.

The Bible talks about a man being the sum of what he thinks.

Say It Ain't So

Proverbs 23:7

For as he thinketh in his heart, so is he: Eat and drink, saith he to thee; but his heart is not with thee.

It is very possible to raise children without the principles in the word of God. People do it all the time. However, raising children alone and doing it with excellence requires guidance from the word of God.

There will be times that are just out of our control. Like who they like as friends, who they will pick as their mates, how they will make future decisions. Again, no matter how a child is raised, they still have the capacity to make the wrong decision given the right set of circumstances.

I believe it is very important to explain that excellence does not mean that you will make no mistakes and that your child or children turned out to be wonderful children with no setbacks or hang-ups. It simply means that you gave it all you had, and when you did not have anything left to give, you allowed God to be God and do the rest.

It is worthy to note God sometimes uses the GPS route— the scenic route, which is the long way around to bring things full circle. I remember when my youngest son was in a place of disappointment and uncertainty. He had broken his arm in his senior year in the last game of the season. He also was not making the grade in his Algebra class which would allow him to go to the college of his choice.

I had to once again let go and let God. Yes, I was actively encouraging and guiding him to do what he needed to do to prepare for college. Getting him from that place of disappointment in his high school football career to a place where he could just say things happen for a reason was unsettling to me because I wasn't sure how he felt about it.

Things did not go exactly how he had envisioned they would. That is life, and single parents deal with not only their life issues but their kid's life issues too.

So I found myself doing the motherly thing by advising and assisting, but I had to sit back and let God be God. I had to pray about how to advise him, what to say to him without making things even worse.

I had to keep myself out of it. I mean, I had to suppress my need to overly express my anxiousness and fear. If I had done things in my own strength and emotions, then I could have consumed him with negative thoughts that could have affected his future in a not-so-good way.

I acknowledge that raising children alone can be done without consulting God, but the question is will that child grow up with drawbacks and bitterness due to the process. It is all about the process. So instead of his focus being on football only, it has shifted seemingly overnight to something totally different. He still loves the game, just in a different way.

The days I spent fussing about him needing to have an interest outside of football are all gone. His focus is now primarily on pleasing God and allowing him to order his steps. When I hear him say, "I am so glad I don't play anymore," and I know he means it, it is priceless.

The message is not that he should not play football but that he overcame every obstacle of the past and is now positioned to step into whatever God has planned for his life and that he is in a happy place.

He did not feel that way until he was forced to look in a new direction. I sat back and said to myself, "Look at God." Amazing things can happen when you let go and let God.

It wasn't easy to see him go through challenge after challenge, knowing that his desire and focus was one thing, and everything happened but that. But because I knew that God had a plan for his life that was much bigger than he would ever dream, bigger than his critics, even bigger than I could imagine.

I had peace that surpassed all understanding. That kind of peace only comes when you let go and trust God to take the wheel. I earnestly can't tell you where my youngest son's future will end up, but I can tell you that God has great plans for him.

No matter what he faces in life, he can look back at that situation and walk out any challenge in excellence. As a single parent, you will face situations that leave you with many questions. My advice to you is to just walk it out.

As I write this, my youngest son has completed his first mission trip and is on his way to becoming a college graduate with hopes of owning his own business one day. The process is still in motion, but I enjoy each victory, no matter how small it may seem.

Letting go means relinquishing your will in the situation, seeking God, and then watching God's will take center stage because the show is all about him, his purpose, and his plan. Sometimes I just think back in amazement on where God has brought me and my family from.

I acknowledge that I have ways to go but also realizing that I have come a long way. Thank you, God.

There is a daily battle that goes on in the minds of all single parents and parents in general, "The Battle of the Letting Go." Your will, your way, how you do things, how you perceive things, how you think, how you treat others and how you view your situation and your future.

Say It Ain't So

Above all, how you view the process of how you are going to get to the next level. The thought of how to transition from raising toddlers to raising elementary-aged children to the middle school age, to high school age, to college age, and then young adulthood. The key is to take one day at a time and savoring each day that you have been given. Enjoying every stage of your children's life. Single parenthood just happens to be your cross, so pick it up and walk with it. No one knows the trials, the letdowns, the disappointments or the struggles of single parenthood unless they have been there. It is not all bad. Absolutely not.

Believe me when I say that there is sunshine after the rain. Now there may not be a pot of gold at the end of the rainbow, but the end of the rainbow itself can become that pot of gold.

I know it is not popular in the culture of today to put our trust in the Creator and want to do everything in our own strength, but when you know that you know how you got over, who can tell you otherwise. So today, I share my "Knowing" with you.

So what I know for sure to be my truth is that God is able, and his dream for us is so much bigger than our dreams for ourselves. Letting go and letting God requires that you trust in him.

Trust that at the end of the day, everything will work itself out. Why? Because when you focus on the bigger picture, it just does. Focusing on what people are saying about your struggle slows you down and frustrates you even more. It causes you to be seated in negative places and not the place of promise.

Let's do a little exercise. Since letting go of the old requires you to take hold of the new, we are going to inhale first. So let's inhale to the max and then exhale slowly. As we are exhaling slowly with our eyes close, we are visualizing all the things in our life that we need to let go of to live on purpose.

Those things that we need to let go of which have delayed our purpose. Those people who have been a distraction or have caused you to feel that you are not worthy to walk boldly and be who you are.

I challenge you to do this exercise as often as you need to. It may not be a one-time all-done situation. The objective is to get to that place where exhaling becomes a no-brainer. The goal is to become so self-aware of who you really are and who God made you to be.

Most of all, as single parents, we need to let go of all the times we made a mistake and fell short of our children's expectations. We need to let go of any failed attempts to always please those around us.

Say It Ain't So

We need to let go of any notion that we need to be a super mom or super dad. We need to let go of any desires to overcompensate for the other parent.

Let go and be free because you cannot do it all. You cannot be all things to all people. You cannot live in the 'what had happened' and press effectively toward the future.

Been There Done That

New Beginnings
Chapter 9 Reflections
'Let It Go'

What do you envision for you and your children's future and how will you get there?

(e.g., a family who value principles, determination, motivation)

1._____

2._____

3._____

4._____

What are you doing to let go of the past and focus on the future?

(e.g., staying away from negativity, speaking positivity)

1._____

2._____

3._____

4._____

Been There Done That

Do you find that letting go of your past is more difficult than concentrating on your future? Why?

1._____

2._____

3._____

4._____

CHAPTER TEN

The Case for the Single Parent

I have heard many people confess parenthood to be the toughest job on the earth. Just think, if parents believe parenting in a two-parent household is difficult, then being a single parent must be at least twice as tough.

Just imagine if both parents in a child's life would check out on them or simply could not be with them most of the time. It would have a major effect on their outlook in life, on families, on communities and the world.

Yes, there are many cases where this happened, and there are statistics to prove unfavorable conditions for all involved. Even if a single parent only could be involved in a child's life half the time, it would leave the child who already has only one involved parent with only half of the other parent's time, attention, guidance and support, which would be truly life-altering.

Single parents should be commended for sticking and staying and never giving up on their children. Someone has to do the heavy lifting, and usually, it is the single mom—no offense, single dads. We are aware many of you are holding down the family also.

Single parents are so important, especially in today's society. If we believe statistics display a world on the brink of disaster due to fatherless children, imagine if the narrative read motherless and fatherless children. Meaning there would be more consequences for children of broken homes which impacts families, communities, society, and the world in a negative way.

We will never really capture the importance of a single mom or a single dad in regards to the trickle-down effect it has on all of society norms.

Single parents are celebrated the less but are the most sacrificial. Single parents have a wealth of knowledge on how to maintain while all the hinges of what is keeping them and their family together are coming off the door. The understanding and partnering with a single parent ensure a pathway to a better future for all of us.

Say It Ain't So

So my hat goes off to all the single parents in the world for your grit and your grind. For smiling when you wanted to cry. For rising early and going to bed late. For standing tall when others tried to take you low.

For standing up when you were told to sit down. For keeping your head up when you were looked down on. For taking all of the brunt of dealing with the emotional roller coaster that's present raising kids.

For looking as if you were keeping it all together when your heart was broken into pieces. For keeping the faith when it seemed hopeless. For loving when you needed love yourself.

For being unselfish and putting your children's future first. For proving the statistics wrong. For believing in yourself and your children. For never letting yourself go. For using every resource, you could find to better your children's future as well as your own. For keeping your dignity even in the tough times. For knowing who you are and that your children had a future. For using tough love when it was required. For being compassionate and kind when you wanted to blow a gasket.

For realizing you do not always know it all. For understanding your children are not perfect. For during without at times because your children had needs. For understanding, if you do all that you can, God would do the rest.

Been There Done That

For trying it just one more time, even with tears in your eyes. For praying when you did not know what else to do. For laughing to keep you from crying.

For supporting others and their children even though you did not know exactly when your breakthrough was going to come.

For believing even though you were in your 'see nothing days.' For not letting a bad day keep you from getting up the next day.

For being so innovative when it was time to improvise because you just had to make do.

For allowing God to heal your heart so that you could be whole and lead your family to wholeness.

For changing the trajectory of the next generation.

For never giving up on your kids. For never giving up on yourself. For never giving up on life.

Thank You, Single Parent!

the heroes of today
Chapter 10 Reflections
'the Case for Single Parents'

Do you agree that single parents are in a unique situation? If yes, why? If no, why not?

1._____

2._____

3._____

4._____

How are you going to turn the lemons (a negative situation) in your life into lemonade (a positive situation)?

(e.g., increase wisdom, increase faith)

1._____

2._____

3._____

4._____

Been There Done That

What do you think are the life lessons in turning challenges into opportunities?

(e.g., nothing is impossible, never quit)

1._____

2._____

3._____

4._____

Letter from the Desk of the Author

*B*lessings! My prayer is that this book blesses your life and lifts you up to your rightful place in God. My prayer is that you will be inspired, encouraged and empowered to take the cards you have been dealt in life and play them with God as your trump card. With God as your trump card, it doesn't matter the hand you were dealt. He makes the difference.

The goal of this book is to first inspire single parents to stretch their faith past what they see. To stretch their faith past what they have experienced. To stretch their faith past what they fear. You being a single parent did not take God by surprise. It may have been a surprise to you, but never God. This means he already has a plan. So, single parents, don't lose your sanity. He has a plan for you as well as your children.

The goal of this book is to also encourage you. There will be many times in your life where you will not find the encouragement you are seeking or needing. At these times, you are going to have to encourage yourself. To be honest, you will encounter many days where this is true. You will find out if you don't encourage yourself, you won't be encouraged to move forth in the purpose God has for you and your family.

Lastly, one of the major goals of this book is to empower you. It is meant to shed light on your right and authority to be moved to action. It doesn't matter where you come from. You have the right to want and seek a better way for you and your children, no matter who thinks differently. You are empowered to shine even if you, or shall I say, especially if you are in a dark place. The word of God comes alongside empowerment and gives you the authority to command any thought, opinion, or behavior to line up with the future God has for you.

Wishing you and your family peace for the journey!

About the Author

Collette Conner is a gifted writer who also has two other completed works. She was a contributor to 'Daily Devotion,' a work in which she was a co-author. She is also the author of "The Little Black Book of Questions, Ten Power Packed Questions Which Will Point You to Your Purpose.' She is a compelling speaker who has inspired many with her unique way of conveying God's love toward single parents. She seeks to inspire, encourage, and empower other single parents to live on purpose.

Collette Conner is a single mom who has raised three sons, Daaven, Brandon, and Kalif. She resides in Houston, TX, where she was born and raised. She credits her spirit and will to overcome any adversities in her life to her faith in God and her belief that purpose most often is birth out of being in a hard place. She believes single parenthood is one of the most challenging tasks in the world but also one of the most important ones. Her passion is to motivate single parents to have a vision for their family and be driven to bring that vision to pass.

Collette is the host of 'Keeping Your Sanity While Single Parenting Podcast.' She is also a Life Coach on MyMentor.life, where she empowers single parents to create and pursue a vision for themselves and their families.

Been There Done That

Collette Conner can be reached for speaking engagements for churches, conferences, retreats, and seminars at <u>ctconner100@gmail.com.</u>

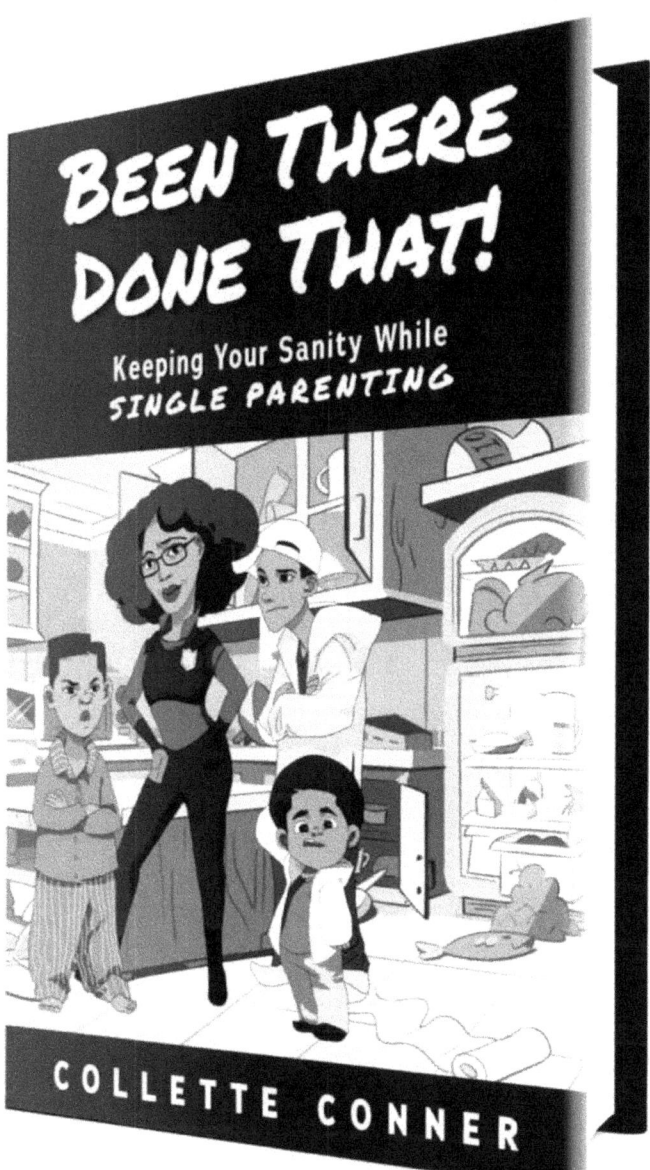

Been There Done That

www.ingramcontent.com/pod-product-compliance
Lightning Source LLC
Chambersburg PA
CBHW071127090426
42736CB00012B/2041